FIND YOUR M[AGIC]

Everyday Journal for Highly Sensitive People

BY: LAUREN R. STEWART

Hi there,

I'm Lauren and I am a highly sensitive person (HSP) like you. I have found that journaling helps me deal with the challenges that come along with being a HSP. It can also help you become creative and uncover your strengths.

I decided to create a journal that you can use every day or whenever you'd like to track your emotions, write down your feelings, keep track of your goals and to-do lists and more.

It is designed specifically for highly sensitive people, but it would be helpful for anyone! Enjoy!

Love,

Lauren

www.findyourmagichsp.com

Today's Date:

 Wakeup time:

 Bedtime:

How do I feel today?

3 things I'm grateful for:

What feels overwhelming? / What can I do about it?

www.findyourmagichsp.com

How can I honor my sensitivity today?

Emotion Tracker (circle how you feel today):

To-Do List:

Goals:

www.findyourmagichsp.com

Today's Date:

 Wakeup time:

 Bedtime:

How do I feel today?

3 things I'm grateful for:

What feels overwhelming? / What can I do about it?

www.findyourmagichsp.com

How can I honor my sensitivity today?

Emotion Tracker (circle how you feel today):

To-Do List:

Goals:

Today's Date:

 Wakeup time:

Bedtime:

How do I feel today?

3 things I'm grateful for:

What feels overwhelming? / What can I do about it?

www.findyourmagichsp.com

How can I honor my sensitivity today?

Emotion Tracker (circle how you feel today):

To-Do List:

Goals:

www.findyourmagichsp.com

Today's Date:

 Wakeup time:

 Bedtime:

How do I feel today?

_____

_____

_____

3 things I'm grateful for:

_____

_____

_____

What feels overwhelming? / What can I do about it?

_____

_____

_____

_____

_____

www.findyourmagichsp.com

How can I honor my sensitivity today?

Emotion Tracker (circle how you feel today):

To-Do List:

Goals:

www.findyourmagichsp.com

Today's Date:

 Wakeup time:

 Bedtime:

How do I feel today?

3 things I'm grateful for:

What feels overwhelming? / What can I do about it?

www.findyourmagicsp.com

How can I honor my sensitivity today?

Emotion Tracker (circle how you feel today):

To-Do List:

Goals:

Today's Date:

 Wakeup time:

 Bedtime:

How do I feel today?

3 things I'm grateful for:

What feels overwhelming? / What can I do about it?

www.findyourmagichsp.com

How can I honor my sensitivity today?

Emotion Tracker (circle how you feel today):

To-Do List:

Goals:

Today's Date:

 Wakeup time:

 Bedtime:

How do I feel today?

3 things I'm grateful for:

What feels overwhelming? / What can I do about it?

www.findyourmagichsp.com

How can I honor my sensitivity today?

Emotion Tracker (circle how you feel today):

To-Do List:

Goals:

Today's Date:

 Wakeup time:

Bedtime:

How do I feel today?

3 things I'm grateful for:

What feels overwhelming? / What can I do about it?

www.findyourmagichsp.com

How can I honor my sensitivity today?

Emotion Tracker (circle how you feel today):

To-Do List:

Goals:

www.findyourmagichsp.com

Today's Date:

 Wakeup time:

 Bedtime:

How do I feel today?

3 things I'm grateful for:

What feels overwhelming? / What can I do about it?

www.findyourmagicsp.com

How can I honor my sensitivity today?

Emotion Tracker (circle how you feel today):

To-Do List:

Goals:

www.findyourmagichsp.com

Today's Date:

 Wakeup time:

 Bedtime:

How do I feel today?

3 things I'm grateful for:

What feels overwhelming? / What can I do about it?

www.findyourmagicsp.com

How can I honor my sensitivity today?

_____

_____

Emotion Tracker (circle how you feel today):

To-Do List:

_____

_____

_____

Goals:

_____

_____

_____

_____

Today's Date:

 Wakeup time:

 Bedtime:

How do I feel today?

_____
_____
_____

3 things I'm grateful for:

_____
_____
_____

What feels overwhelming? / What can I do about it?

_____
_____
_____
_____
_____

www.findyourmagichsp.com

How can I honor my sensitivity today?

Emotion Tracker (circle how you feel today):

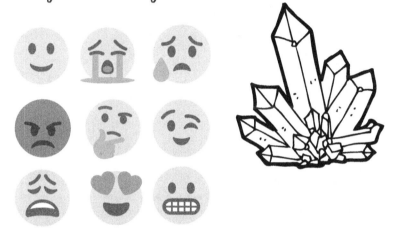

To-Do List:

Goals:

www.findyourmagichsp.com

Today's Date:

 Wakeup time:

 Bedtime:

How do I feel today?

3 things I'm grateful for:

What feels overwhelming? / What can I do about it?

How can I honor my sensitivity today?

Emotion Tracker (circle how you feel today):

To-Do List:

Goals:

Today's Date:

 Wakeup time:

 Bedtime:

How do I feel today?

3 things I'm grateful for:

What feels overwhelming? / What can I do about it?

www.findyourmagicsp.com

How can I honor my sensitivity today?

Emotion Tracker (circle how you feel today):

To-Do List:

Goals:

www.findyourmagichsp.com

Today's Date:

 Wakeup time:

 Bedtime:

How do I feel today?

3 things I'm grateful for:

What feels overwhelming? / What can I do about it?

www.findyourmagichsp.com

How can I honor my sensitivity today?

_____

_____

Emotion Tracker (circle how you feel today):

To-Do List:

_____

_____

_____

Goals:

_____

_____

_____

Today's Date:

 Wakeup time:

Bedtime:

How do I feel today?

3 things I'm grateful for:

What feels overwhelming? / What can I do about it?

www.findyourmagicsp.com

How can I honor my sensitivity today?

Emotion Tracker (circle how you feel today):

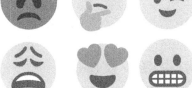

To-Do List:

Goals:

www.findyourmagichsp.com

Today's Date:

 Wakeup time:

 Bedtime:

How do I feel today?

3 things I'm grateful for:

What feels overwhelming? / What can I do about it?

www.findyourmagicsp.com

How can I honor my sensitivity today?

Emotion Tracker (circle how you feel today):

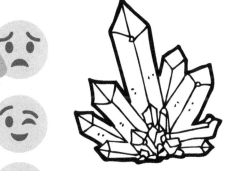

To-Do List:

Goals:

www.findyourmagichsp.com

Today's Date:

 Wakeup time:

 Bedtime:

How do I feel today?

3 things I'm grateful for:

What feels overwhelming? / What can I do about it?

www.findyourmagicsp.com

How can I honor my sensitivity today?

Emotion Tracker (circle how you feel today):

To-Do List:

Goals:

www.findyourmagichsp.com

Today's Date:

 Wakeup time:

 Bedtime:

How do I feel today?

3 things I'm grateful for:

What feels overwhelming? / What can I do about it?

www.findyourmagicsp.com

How can I honor my sensitivity today?

_____

_____

_____

Emotion Tracker (circle how you feel today):

To-Do List:

Goals:

_____

_____

_____

_____

Today's Date:

 Wakeup time:

 Bedtime:

How do I feel today?

3 things I'm grateful for:

What feels overwhelming? / What can I do about it?

www.findyourmagicsp.com

How can I honor my sensitivity today?

Emotion Tracker (circle how you feel today):

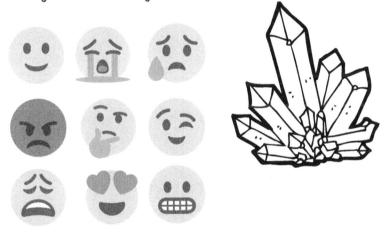

To-Do List:

Goals:

Today's Date:

 Wakeup time:

 Bedtime:

How do I feel today?

3 things I'm grateful for:

What feels overwhelming? / What can I do about it?

www.findyourmagichsp.com

How can I honor my sensitivity today?

Emotion Tracker (circle how you feel today):

To-Do List:

Goals:

www.findyourmagichsp.com

Today's Date:

 Wakeup time:

 Bedtime:

How do I feel today?

3 things I'm grateful for:

What feels overwhelming? / What can I do about it?

www.findyourmagichsp.com

How can I honor my sensitivity today?

Emotion Tracker (circle how you feel today):

To-Do List:

Goals:

Today's Date:

 Wakeup time:

 Bedtime:

How do I feel today?

3 things I'm grateful for:

What feels overwhelming? / What can I do about it?

www.findyourmagichsp.com

How can I honor my sensitivity today?

Emotion Tracker (circle how you feel today):

To-Do List:

Goals:

www.findyourmagichsp.com

Today's Date:

 Wakeup time:

 Bedtime:

How do I feel today?

3 things I'm grateful for:

What feels overwhelming? / What can I do about it?

www.findyourmagicsp.com

How can I honor my sensitivity today?

Emotion Tracker (circle how you feel today):

To-Do List:

Goals:

Today's Date:

 Wakeup time:

 Bedtime:

How do I feel today?

_____

_____

_____

3 things I'm grateful for:

_____

_____

_____

What feels overwhelming? / What can I do about it?

_____

_____

_____

_____

_____

www.findyourmagicksp.com

How can I honor my sensitivity today?

Emotion Tracker (circle how you feel today):

To-Do List:

Goals:

www.findyourmagichsp.com

Today's Date:

 Wakeup time:

 Bedtime:

How do I feel today?

3 things I'm grateful for:

What feels overwhelming? / What can I do about it?

www.findyourmagichsp.com

How can I honor my sensitivity today?

Emotion Tracker (circle how you feel today):

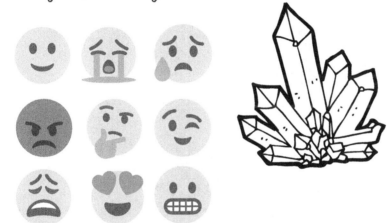

To-Do List:

Goals:

Today's Date:

 Wakeup time:

 Bedtime:

How do I feel today?

3 things I'm grateful for:

What feels overwhelming? / What can I do about it?

www.findyourmagichsp.com

How can I honor my sensitivity today?

Emotion Tracker (circle how you feel today):

To-Do List:

Goals:

www.findyourmagichsp.com

Today's Date:

 Wakeup time:

 Bedtime:

How do I feel today?

3 things I'm grateful for:

What feels overwhelming? / What can I do about it?

www.findyourmagichsp.com

How can I honor my sensitivity today?

Emotion Tracker (circle how you feel today):

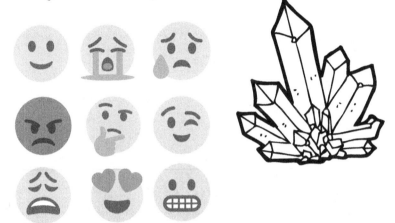

To-Do List:

Goals:

www.findyourmagichsp.com

Today's Date:

 Wakeup time:

 Bedtime:

How do I feel today?

3 things I'm grateful for:

What feels overwhelming? / What can I do about it?

www.findyourmagichsp.com

How can I honor my sensitivity today?

_____

_____

_____

Emotion Tracker (circle how you feel today):

To-Do List:

_____

_____

_____

_____

Goals:

_____

_____

_____

_____

Today's Date:

 Wakeup time:

Bedtime:

How do I feel today?

3 things I'm grateful for:

What feels overwhelming? / What can I do about it?

How can I honor my sensitivity today?

Emotion Tracker (circle how you feel today):

To-Do List:

Goals:

Today's Date:

 Wakeup time:

 Bedtime:

How do I feel today?

3 things I'm grateful for:

What feels overwhelming? / What can I do about it?

www.findyourmagicsp.com

How can I honor my sensitivity today?

Emotion Tracker (circle how you feel today):

To-Do List:

Goals:

Today's Date:

 Wakeup time:

 Bedtime:

How do I feel today?

3 things I'm grateful for:

What feels overwhelming? / What can I do about it?

www.findyourmagichsp.com

How can I honor my sensitivity today?

Emotion Tracker (circle how you feel today):

To-Do List:

Goals:

Today's Date:

 Wakeup time:

Bedtime:

How do I feel today?
___
___
___

3 things I'm grateful for:
___
___
___

What feels overwhelming? / What can I do about it?

___
___
___
___
___
___

www.findyourmagichsp.com

How can I honor my sensitivity today?

_____

_____

_____

Emotion Tracker (circle how you feel today):

To-Do List:

_____

_____

_____

Goals:

_____

_____

_____

_____

www.findyourmagichsp.com

Today's Date:

 Wakeup time:

 Bedtime:

How do I feel today?

3 things I'm grateful for:

What feels overwhelming? / What can I do about it?

www.findyourmagichsp.com

How can I honor my sensitivity today?

Emotion Tracker (circle how you feel today):

To-Do List:

Goals:

www.findyourmagichsp.com

Today's Date:

 Wakeup time:

 Bedtime:

How do I feel today?

3 things I'm grateful for:

What feels overwhelming? / What can I do about it?

www.findyourmagicsp.com

How can I honor my sensitivity today?

Emotion Tracker (circle how you feel today):

To-Do List:

Goals:

www.findyourmagichsp.com

Today's Date:

 Wakeup time:

 Bedtime:

How do I feel today?

3 things I'm grateful for:

What feels overwhelming? / What can I do about it?

www.findyourmagicshp.com

How can I honor my sensitivity today?

Emotion Tracker (circle how you feel today):

To-Do List:

Goals:

www.findyourmagichsp.com

Today's Date:

 Wakeup time:

 Bedtime:

How do I feel today?

3 things I'm grateful for:

What feels overwhelming? / What can I do about it?

www.findyourmagichsp.com

How can I honor my sensitivity today?

_____
_____
_____

Emotion Tracker (circle how you feel today):

To-Do List:
_____
_____
_____
_____

Goals:
_____
_____
_____
_____
_____

Today's Date:

 Wakeup time:

Bedtime:

How do I feel today?

3 things I'm grateful for:

What feels overwhelming? / What can I do about it?

www.findyourmagicksp.com

How can I honor my sensitivity today?

Emotion Tracker (circle how you feel today):

To-Do List:

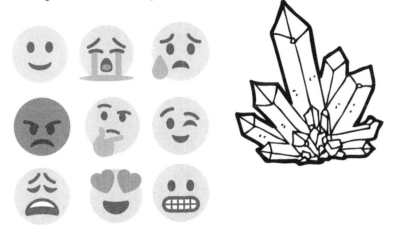

Goals:

Today's Date:

 Wakeup time:

 Bedtime:

How do I feel today?

3 things I'm grateful for:

_____

_____

_____

_____

What feels overwhelming? / What can I do about it?

_____

_____

_____

_____

_____

_____

www.findyourmagichsp.com

How can I honor my sensitivity today?

Emotion Tracker (circle how you feel today):

To-Do List:

Goals:

www.findyourmagichsp.com

Today's Date:

 Wakeup time:

 Bedtime:

How do I feel today?

3 things I'm grateful for:

What feels overwhelming? / What can I do about it?

www.findyourmagichsp.com

How can I honor my sensitivity today?

Emotion Tracker (circle how you feel today):

To-Do List:

Goals:

www.findyourmagichsp.com

Today's Date:

 Wakeup time:

 Bedtime:

How do I feel today?

3 things I'm grateful for:

What feels overwhelming? / What can I do about it?

www.findyourmagichsp.com

How can I honor my sensitivity today?

Emotion Tracker (circle how you feel today):

To-Do List:

Goals:

www.findyourmagichsp.com

Today's Date:

 Wakeup time:

 Bedtime:

How do I feel today?

3 things I'm grateful for:

What feels overwhelming? / What can I do about it?

www.findyourmagichsp.com

How can I honor my sensitivity today?

Emotion Tracker (circle how you feel today):

To-Do List:

Goals:

Today's Date:

 Wakeup time:

 Bedtime:

How do I feel today?

3 things I'm grateful for:

What feels overwhelming? / What can I do about it?

www.findyourmagichsp.com

How can I honor my sensitivity today?

Emotion Tracker (circle how you feel today):

To-Do List:

Goals:

www.findyourmagichsp.com

Today's Date:

 Wakeup time:

 Bedtime:

How do I feel today?

3 things I'm grateful for:

What feels overwhelming? / What can I do about it?

www.findyourmagichsp.com

How can I honor my sensitivity today?

Emotion Tracker (circle how you feel today):

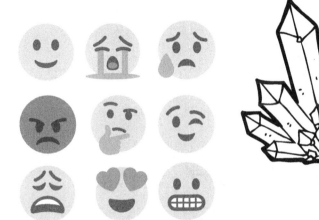

To-Do List:

Goals:

www.findyourmagichsp.com

Today's Date:

 Wakeup time:

 Bedtime:

How do I feel today?

3 things I'm grateful for:

What feels overwhelming? / What can I do about it?

www.findyourmagicsp.com

How can I honor my sensitivity today?

_____

_____

Emotion Tracker (circle how you feel today):

To-Do List:

_____

_____

_____

_____

Goals:

_____

_____

_____

_____

Today's Date:

 Wakeup time:

 Bedtime:

How do I feel today?

3 things I'm grateful for:

What feels overwhelming? / What can I do about it?

www.findyourmagicsp.com

How can I honor my sensitivity today?

Emotion Tracker (circle how you feel today):

To-Do List:

Goals:

www.findyourmagichsp.com

Today's Date:

 Wakeup time:

 Bedtime:

How do I feel today?

_____

_____

_____

3 things I'm grateful for:

_____

_____

_____

What feels overwhelming? / What can I do about it?

_____

_____

_____

_____

_____

_____

www.findyourmagicsp.com

How can I honor my sensitivity today?

Emotion Tracker (circle how you feel today):

To-Do List:

Goals:

Today's Date:

 Wakeup time:

 Bedtime:

How do I feel today?

3 things I'm grateful for:

What feels overwhelming? / What can I do about it?

www.findyourmagichsp.com

How can I honor my sensitivity today?

Emotion Tracker (circle how you feel today):

To-Do List:

Goals:

Today's Date:

 Wakeup time:

 Bedtime:

How do I feel today?
_____
_____
_____
_____

3 things I'm grateful for:
_____
_____
_____
_____

What feels overwhelming? / What can I do about it?

_____
_____
_____
_____
_____

www.findyourmagichsp.com

How can I honor my sensitivity today?

Emotion Tracker (circle how you feel today):

To-Do List:

Goals:

www.findyourmagichsp.com

Today's Date:

 Wakeup time:

 Bedtime:

How do I feel today?

3 things I'm grateful for:

What feels overwhelming? / What can I do about it?

www.findyourmagicksp.com

How can I honor my sensitivity today?

Emotion Tracker (circle how you feel today):

To-Do List:

Goals:

www.findyourmagichsp.com

Today's Date:

 Wakeup time:

 Bedtime:

How do I feel today?

3 things I'm grateful for:

What feels overwhelming? / What can I do about it?

www.findyourmagichsp.com

How can I honor my sensitivity today?

Emotion Tracker (circle how you feel today):

To-Do List:

Goals:

Today's Date:

 Wakeup time:

 Bedtime:

How do I feel today?

3 things I'm grateful for:

What feels overwhelming? / What can I do about it?

www.findyourmagicsp.com

How can I honor my sensitivity today?

Emotion Tracker (circle how you feel today):

To-Do List:

Goals:

Today's Date:

 Wakeup time:

 Bedtime:

How do I feel today?

3 things I'm grateful for:

What feels overwhelming? / What can I do about it?

www.findyourmagicsp.com

How can I honor my sensitivity today?

Emotion Tracker (circle how you feel today):

To-Do List:

Goals:

Made in the USA
Columbia, SC
25 November 2020